LAKE VILLA DISTRICT LIBRARY

3 1981 00527 8092

D1552164

DO BEES POOP?

Learning about Living and Nonliving Things with
THE GARBAGE GANG

LAKE VILLA DISTRICT LIBRARY
1001 East Grand Avenue
Lake Villa, IL 60046-9154
(847) 356-7711

by Thomas Kingsley Troupe   Illustrated by Derek Toye

PICTURE WINDOW BOOKS
a capstone imprint

MEET THE GARBAGE GANG:

SAM HAMMWICH

Sam is a once-delicious sandwich that has a bit of lettuce and tomato. He is usually crabby and a bit of a loudmouth.

GORDY

Gordy is a small rhino who wears an eyepatch even though he doesn't need one. He lives in the city dump. His friends don't visit him in the smelly dump, so Gordy created his own friends—the Garbage Gang!

SOGGY

Soggy is a stuffed bear from a carnival game. She fell into a puddle of dumpster juice and has never been the same.

RICK

Rick is a brick. He is terrified of bugs, especially bees, which is odd . . . since he's a brick.

CANN-DEE

Cann-Dee is a robot made of aluminum cans. She can pull random facts out of thin air.

MR. FRIGID

Mr. Frigid is a huge refrigerator that sprouted arms and legs. He doesn't say much, but he's super strong.

Oh, no! Not bees! Open up Mr. Frigid, I'm outta here!

6

I think all living things poop, guys. That's what happens when you eat stuff.

CRUNCH!

Your theory computes, Gordon. Creatures that eat produce a waste product. And some living things store their waste inside their own bodies.

Like their own internal garbage dump?

Affirmative.

Please don't put our hive there, fridge guy.

Oooh. Look at the little kitty sleeping!

Oh, yeah, that's another thing that living things do.

Get fur all over a broken down old stove?

No, Sam. Living things rest.

It's true. Living things are born, live for a while, but will later die.

What a bunch of garbage!

Incoming data indicates all creatures have a limited lifespan.

Some bees die after stinging humans.

Bummer.

That's terrible!

Yeah, but when living things die, they make room for more living things.

Glossary

exhaust—the waste gases made by an engine

extinct—when a species of creature has died off

frigid—super cold

internal—something that is kept inside

processor—something that carries out a number of different operations

reproduce—to make its own kind

sassy—acting somewhat rude

theory—an idea using facts to support it

vomit—to throw up food and liquid from your stomach through your mouth

You're looking up words? That's one smart move, kid!

Read More

Braun, Eric. *Gertrude and Reginald the Monsters Talk about Living and Nonliving.* In the Science Lab. North Mankato, Minn.: Capstone, 2012.

Hicks, Kelli. *Living or Non-Living?* Vero Beach, Fla.: Rourke Publishing, 2011.

Kalman, Bobbie. *What Kind of Living Thing Is It?* New York: Crabtree Publishing, 2010.

My sensors indicate that books are just as sweet as honey!

Critical Thinking Using the Common Core

1. There are differences between living and nonliving things. Can you name three of them? (Key Ideas and Details)

2. Living things die to make way for other living things. Do nonliving things remain forever? Look online and check written sources to find an answer. (Integration of Knowledge and Ideas)

Index

Internet Sites

FactHound offers a safe, fun way to find Internet sites related to this book. All of the sites on FactHound have been researched by our staff.

Here's all you do:

Visit *www.facthound.com*

Type in this code: 9781479554775

Super-cool stuff! Check out projects, games and lots more at **www.capstonekids.com**

Thanks to our advisers for their expertise, research, and advice:
Christopher T. Ruhland, PhD
Professor of Biological Sciences
Department of Biology
Minnesota State University, Mankato

Terry Flaherty, PhD, Professor of English
Minnesota State University, Mankato

Editor: Shelly Lyons
Designer: Lori Bye
Art Director: Nathan Gassman
Production Specialist: Gene Bentdahl
The illustrations in this book were created digitally
Picture Window Books are published by Capstone,
1710 Roe Crest Drive, North Mankato, Minnesota 56003
www.capstonepub.com

Copyright © 2015 by Picture Window Books, a Capstone imprint. All rights reserved. No part of this publication may be reproduced in whole or in part, or stored in a retrieval system, or transmitted in any form or by any means, electronic, mechanical, photocopying, recording, or otherwise, without written permission of the publisher.

Library of Congress Cataloging-in-Publication Data
Troupe, Thomas Kingsley, author.
Do bees poop? : learning about living and nonliving things with the Garbage Gang / by Thomas Kingsley Troupe ; illustrated by Derek Toye.
pages cm. — (Nonfiction picture books. The Garbage Gang's super science questions)
Summary: "Humorous text and characters teach kids all about living and nonliving things"—Provided by publisher.
Audience: Ages 5–7.
Audience: K to grade 3.
Includes bibliographical references and index.
ISBN 978-1-4795-5477-5 (library binding)
ISBN 978-1-4795-5485-0 (eBook PDF)
1. Life (Biology)—Juvenile literature. 2. Honeybee—Juvenile literature.
I. Toye, Derek, illustrator. II. Title.
QH501.T72 2015
570—dc23   2014001529
Printed in the United States of America in North Mankato, Minnesota
032014   008087CGF14

Look for all the books in the series:

DO ANTS GET LOST? Learning about Animal Communication with **THE GARBAGE GANG**

DO BEES POOP? Learning about Living and Nonliving Things with **THE GARBAGE GANG**

WHY DO DEAD FISH FLOAT? Learning about Matter with **THE GARBAGE GANG**

WHY DOES MY BODY MAKE BUBBLES? Learning about the Digestive System with **THE GARBAGE GANG**